Reggie the Rescue Dog

Dedicated to those who work tirelessly to rescue and rehome animals in need.

And to second chances.

Gina Dawson

Reggie
THE RESCUE DOG

Gina Dawson

Illustrated by
Bima Perera

Dad, Angus and Elsa have moved in with Grandma. There's room for everyone in Grandma's big house, but best of all, there's lots of land outside.

"Plenty of room for a dog," says Dad with a grin.

"Yay!" yells Elsa.

"At last!" says Angus.

"Before we had no space and were way too busy to look after a dog properly," says Dad. "Dogs need exercise, training and care."

"I'll help!" says Elsa, excitedly.

"Me too," says Angus.

Grandma adds, "I'm home a lot so I'll help too. Dogs are good company."

Dad says, "So next we need to find the right dog for our family."

"What about a rescue dog?" says Grandma. "Perhaps we can rescue a dog that needs a good home and a second chance."

Next morning at the shelter they see many dogs waiting for new homes.

"How do we choose?" asks Elsa sadly.

Shelley the shelter lady asks many questions. Then she says, "You are an active family with lots of space. I may have the right dog for you."

Soon she is back.

"Her name is Reggie," Shelley says.

"She looks sad," says Elsa.

"She's scared," says Shelley.

"Reggie was kept inside every day. She has loads of energy, but she never had walks or lessons, and she was lonely and bored. She found things to eat and to play with, and every night her owners grew angrier and angrier. Reggie didn't understand why. She only wanted some fun! Now she's here, needing a home."

"Dreadful," says Grandma.

"Reggie is healthy and gentle.
She'll need help learning to trust
people again, and to behave nicely."

"We'd love to adopt Reggie,"
says Dad, and everyone smiles.

That afternoon they shop and prepare the house and yard, and the next morning Dad collects Reggie. Soon she is exploring her new home. She jumps at strange sounds, and soon scurries into her kennel.

"She feels safer there," says Grandma. "We'll let her settle in."

Hours later, Reggie's tummy is rumbling. Her nose twitches when Angus brings a bowl of food, and soon she is gulping her meal, licking her bowl clean.

Later they go walking. Reggie pulls on her lead, barks at dogs and jumps in fright at a passing car. Dad holds the lead tightly.

"Outside is strange and scary for Reggie," Dad says. "We must keep her safe while she learns."

Everyone pitches in to look after Reggie, and soon she seems happier and not so scared.

But Reggie's tail doesn't wag.

Every morning, Elsa gives Reggie breakfast and fresh water.
In the day, Grandma talks to her and keeps her busy, so she
never gets bored.

After school, Angus takes her for a walk and gives her dinner.

Dad brushes her and teaches her to play ball. Every evening, Reggie comes inside and learns to be a well-mannered indoor dog.

Each Saturday is obedience school. Angus and Reggie learn together. Angus praises Reggie when she does well. Reggie meets other dogs and learns to greet them politely. Best of all, Reggie loves pleasing Angus, and sometimes her tail almost wags.

Every day, Angus and Reggie practise their lessons. Soon Reggie can sit, stay, come when she's called and walk calmly on her lead.

At the end of summer is exam day.

Everyone holds their breath as Reggie
and Angus complete their tasks.

When Reggie passes her test Trevor the trainer is pleased.
"Rescue dogs sometimes need extra help, but you've done
an amazing job with Reggie," Trevor says.

Everyone smiles and Grandma cries a happy tear.

One wintery afternoon, Dad, Angus and Elsa arrive home from sport. The house is cold and dark, and Grandma and Reggie aren't there.

"Grandma wouldn't go out on a day like this," says Dad worriedly.

Elsa says, "There's Grandma's phone."

"Listen," says Angus.

A dog is barking.

"That's Reggie," says Dad, and they see Reggie running towards them. Then she runs back the way she came.

"She wants us to follow," says Angus. They cross the slippery grass and find a damp and muddy Grandma inside the shed.

"I was picking vegetables," she says. "I slipped and hurt my ankle. Then it rained. Reggie helped me under cover."

"You must be freezing," says Dad. "Let's get you to the house."

"I'm not cold," says Grandma. "Reggie laid on me all day and kept me warm. When she heard the car, she went to fetch you."

That night they sit around the crackling fire.

"Reggie is part of our family now," says Elsa.

"Yes," agrees Dad, "I'm proud of how we've all helped look after Reggie. We've given her a loving home."

"Reggie the rescue dog," says Angus.

"We rescued Reggie, but Reggie also rescued us," says Grandma. "She makes us laugh, keeps us fit, and is great company. Now she even looks after us!"

And Reggie's tail wags.

Gina Dawson is the author of several children's books about dogs with jobs. She has also authored books about a variety of social issues for young readers. Before retiring to write, Gina was an educator and counsellor, presenting programs on a variety of social issues in schools. She is a lifelong lover of dogs, a volunteer to an assistance dog organisation, and an experienced trainer. When she is not researching, writing or dreaming up new ideas, Gina ghost writes memoirs for adults, along with the occasional short story. Outside of writing she has a diverse range of interests and a long bucket list. She lives with her husband Jim and their dynamic dog, Kiera. *Reggie the Rescue Dog* and *Lester the Library Dog* are her twelfth and thirteenth books. More about Gina's work can be found at www.ginadawson.com.

Bima Perera is an Australian illustrator residing in the bustling city of Tokyo. Born in Japan to Sri Lankan parents and raised in Brisbane, she grew up across multiple cultural settings, where language sometimes became a barrier. This experience enhanced her ability to communicate visually through her drawings. Bima primarily works with gouache paint. She loves the warmth and nostalgia of the traditional medium, and hopes her illustrations will bring you back to those cosy feelings from your childhood days.

When she isn't painting, she enjoys cooking and illustrating her recipes, holding art classes for kids, and exploring the Japanese countryside with her husband and their adorable rescue dog, Billie.

You can see more of her work at www.bimaillustration.com.

Other recent working dog titles by Gina Dawson

Lester

THE LIBRARY DOG

Gina Dawson

Illustrated by
Bima Perera

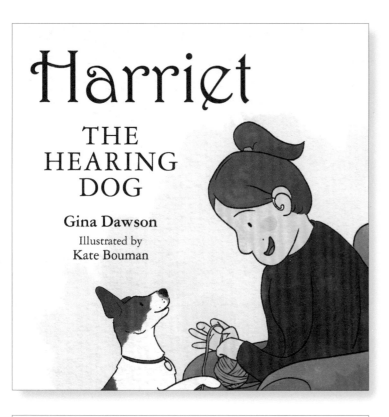

Harriet
THE HEARING DOG

Gina Dawson

Illustrated by
Kate Bouman

Gus
THE GUIDE DOG

Gina Dawson

Illustrated by
Kate Bouman

STOP - 118

First published in 2023 by New Holland Publishers
Sydney • Auckland

Level 1, 178 Fox Valley Road, Wahroonga, NSW 2076, Australia

newhollandpublishers.com

A record of this book is held at the National Library of Australia.

ISBN 9781760795221

Group Managing Director: Fiona Schultz
Project Editor: Liz Hardy
Designer: Andrew Davies
Production Director: Arlene Gippert
Printed in China

10 9 8 7 6 5 4 3 2 1

Keep up with New Holland Publishers:

 NewHollandPublishers

 @newhollandpublishers